Hikes with Tykes: Games and Activities

By Rob Bignell

HIKES WITH TYKES: GAMES AND ACTIVTIES

Copyright Rob Bignell, 2012

Atiswinic Press
Ojai, Calif. 93023
http://hikeswithtykes.com/home.html

ISBN 978-0-9858739-0-5
Library of Congress Control Number: 2012912401

Cover photos by Rob Bignell

Manufactured in the United States of America
First printing July 2012

For Kieran

ACKNOWLEDGEMENTS

Thank you to all of the parents and colleagues
who contributed tips and advice.

Table of Contents

Introduction

You haven't walked more than a hundred yards on the trail when your middle child says, "I'm bored." Bored? How could anyone be bored walking beneath a canopy of trees that looks like it's out of a fairy tale? "The cool rocks are just up ahead," you tell him. He groans.

You reach the cool rocks. That's when your eldest child starts climbing up the granite formation and jumping off the first ledge one story up. You admonish him, tell him to never do that again. Then you have to tell your middle child to get down. He rolls his eyes before doing what you've asked.

Moving beyond the granite rocks, your youngest child complains that his legs hurt. You tell him the picnic area isn't only a little farther. Your middle child says, "Let's eat now!"

It's the day hike from your nightmares.

Most children will find fun the idea of a hike and explore. Still, kids can be fickle creatures. Their lack of knowledge and experience in the world often makes them cautious about suggested activities. And in today's video game-oriented, 300-cable channel, Internet-connected world, some kids may be reluctant – or even afraid – to get outside.

You want to sway kids to at least entertain the notion

that a hike might be fun. If they hit the trail thinking a long stretch of boredom awaits them, they'll make the experience miserable for both themselves and for you.

One step that moms, dads or grandparents can take to get their kids excited about being outside is through games and activities played on the trail. In my first book, "Hikes with Tykes: A Practical Guide to Day Hiking with Children," I listed a number of games and activities for the hike. Since then, parents across the nation have sent me additional suggestions, and as my son grew older, I found myself devising a few more. This book compiles all of those great games and activities that can lead to the day hike of your dreams.

Good reason to have fun

There are quite a number of good reasons to engage kids in games and activities when hiking.

First and foremost is the bonding experience it provides. For some children, especially those who already enjoy a strong relationship with their parents, simply being with mom or dad on a hike may be enough. But often it isn't; instead, child and parent (or grandparent or guardian) must interact. They forge an unbreakable bond with one another when they share experiences. Games and activities on a hike can become those experiences that children fondly remember years from now – or they may be the ice breaker that provides the child with enough comfort to later broach difficult subjects with you.

Many games and activities played on the hiking trail can increase a child's knowledge and understanding of the natural world. From making bark rubbings to identifying animal tracks, from becoming more observant in a scavenger hunt to being the assistant map reader, games and activities geared toward nature and the environment can establish a life-long love for Mother Nature and her wonders. The great outdoors is a whole new, even alien, world for children to discover. Certain games and activities on a hike can prod them toward exploring it.

On a broader scope, many hiking games and activities can develop a child's cognitive, physical and creative skills. Solving word puzzles and geocaching, walking like an animal and rock climbing, drawing and journaling, all can develop a child's abilities and talents in fun ways and in a unique environment at that. Many children won't even realize they're learning.

Ultimately, games and activities can keep kids from getting bored. Some children just won't appreciate the beauty of the trail (at least not at first) or will argue that the walk is too long (Usually they realize this when your destination is less distant than turning back!). A competition or singing camp songs will take their mind off their boredom or tired legs. This can help maintain an adult's sanity, as you then don't have to put up with parent-nag (You know, when kids say, "I'm hungry," "Are we almost there?" or "I have to go to the bathroom."). In the long run, games and activities on the trail not only can make the hike more enjoyable but even can cause children to want to go on more hikes.

New age, new game

The types of games and activities you select for a day hike with kids – or if you select any at all – depend largely upon the child's age. That's because as children grow, their interactions with you and with nature change.

Infants in baby carriers largely are passive passengers. While you must be aware of and tend to their needs as you would any infant, no special games or activities really are necessary for the trail. They'll be happy to see the sights around them, play with the back of your sun hat, and sleep in the gentle breeze created by your steady pace.

For my son, that passivity changed sometime after he turned one when he began to string together words into sentences and started talking with me. His passivity totally ended when he came down from the carrier sometime during his third year. Toddlers in the carrier generally are easy to amuse with songs and simply pointing out the names of various trees, birds and other objects in nature. To them, the outdoors is still all brand new. Once toddlers begin walking on their own and reach their preschool years, however, they'll flit from point to point, touching and examining everything around them. Engagement with them becomes increasingly important so that they behave and do not become bored. This is an excellent opportunity for adults to employ games and activities that build their skills and love for nature while strengthening the parent-child bond.

Most elementary school kids generally are able to amuse themselves, especially if a friend comes along on the hike, but you shouldn't pass on this chance to continue developing their cognitive, observational and creative skills. The games now can become more sophisticated, and they'll likely want to play a variety of them (unlike the preschooler who usually likes to do the same game over and over). Interacting with your child remains as important as ever so you can lay a good foundation to ensure meaningful communication is possible during coming teen years.

Teenagers gradually will become more interested in the destination rather than the journey, taking a more adult view of hiking. They still will enjoy games and activities but are likely to be more selective about what they play. Most will prefer activities that revolve around their interests, such as drawing or journaling. A good way to keep teens involved in the hike and interacting with you is to give them leadership roles and responsibilities: Allow them to select the trail, to help plan the trip, to navigate during the hike, to locate rest spots. You're now developing their hiking skills and teaching them the fundamentals of the sport so that once they become adults, they will be excellent hikers – who in turn take their own children down long trails into the wilds.

Different portions of the hike

As I've talked over the years with fellow parent hikers, I've been given a lot of different suggestions about games and activities for the trail. This book collects those various games and activities, many of which I tried with my own son or have seen in action as our families hiked together.

Because the games and activities that children are capable of playing (let alone interested in playing!) vary with age, the entries are listed by age appropriateness from youngest to oldest. The appropriateness for each game and activity is only an approximation, of course, as each child develops at a different pace. You'll find the age listed at the end of each entry.

The games and activities further are divided into three sections:

■ **Pre-hike games and activities** – Some children may not be that excited about hitting the hiking trail. These games and activities focus on what you can do beforehand to kindle their interest. There's also a brief section about games and activities that can be played on the long drive to the trailhead.

■ **During the hike games and activities** – The bulk of the games and activities in this book are for when you're on the trail. They are separated into two categories: those that foster an awareness of and love for nature and those that are merely fun ways to pass the time.

■ **Post-hike games and activities** – Upon returning home, you can "review" the hike in kid-friendly ways. This will help keep kid's enthusiasm charged for the next adventure.

You'll likely recognize many of the games here, as you played them on hikes, camping trips, and school bus rides when you were a child. Besides giving you new ideas, hopefully they'll jog your memory so you'll remember other games, not listed here, that you played as a child. One of the greatest gifts you can give your child is the sharing of those games and activities that you played when young. They will become fond memories for both you and your child...and years from now, your legacy will be passed on for once grown up he will teach those games and activities to his own children as well.

Special Section: How to Hike with Kids

When I began hiking with my son, he was but four months old. I dressed him warmly and stuck him in the baby carrier then packed an extra diaper and some milk in a bottle. I thought myself pretty smart.

But when time came to change his diaper on the trail, I realized I had no pad to lay my son on. I improvised, placing my jacket between him and the wet ground. Another mile down the trail, we ran out of milk.

As my son grew older, I quickly realized that he hiked quite differently than me and had entirely different needs on the trail. And as I studied first-aid techniques, I came to understand that children's injuries had to be treated differently than adults. If I'd done CPR on my son as I'd been trained to in the army, I'd probably have broken his ribs.

The simply reality is that hiking with children requires unique knowledge that backpacking guidebooks at best skirt over.

Attitude Adjustment

To enjoy hiking with kids, you'll first have to adopt your child's perspective. Simply put, we must learn to hike on our kids' schedules – even though they may not know that's what we're doing.

Compared to adults, kids can't walk as far, they can't walk as fast, and they will grow bored more quickly. Every step we take requires three for them. In addition, early walkers, up to 2 years of age, prefer to wander rather than "hike." Preschool kids will start to walk the trail, but at a rate of only about a mile per hour. With stops, that can turn a three-mile hike into a four-hour journey. Kids also won't be able to hike as steep of trails as you or handle as inclement of weather as you might.

This all may sound limiting, especially to long-time backpackers used to racking up miles or bagging peaks on their hikes, but it's really not. While you may have to put off some backcountry and mountain climbing trips for a while, it also opens up to you a number of great short trails and nature hikes with spectacular sights that you may have otherwise skipped because they weren't challenging enough.

So sure, you'll have to make some compromises, but the payout is high. You're not personally on the hike to get a workout but to spend quality time with your children.

Preparing for the hike

You'll get more out of the hike if you research it and plan ahead. It's not enough to just pull over to the side of the road and hit a trail that you've never been on and have no idea where it goes. In fact, doing so invites disaster.

When selecting a destination, remember that not all kids are made alike. The five-year-old neighbor boy may have had no trouble with a specific trail, but your five-year-old may not like it or be able to handle it. There's nothing wrong with that. We're all different and develop at our own rates.

For your first few hikes, stick to short, well-known trails where you're likely to encounter others. Once you get a feel for hiking and your kids' abilities and interests, expand to longer and more remote trails.

Until they enter their late teens, children need to stick to trails rather than going off-trail hiking, which is known as bushwhacking. Children too easily can get lost when off trail. They also can easily get scratched and cut up or stumble across poisonous plants and dangerous animals.

Always check to see what the weather will be like on the trail you plan to hike. While an adult might be able to withstand wind and a sprinkle here or there, for children it can be pure misery. Dry, pleasantly warm days with limited wind always are best when hiking with children.

Don't choose a trail that is any longer than the youngest child in your group can hike. Adults in good shape can go 8-12 miles a day; for kids, it's much less. There's no magical number. Ask other parents what their children can do, and you'll get a whole range of answers. The reality is that every child is different: different leg lengths, different attitudes toward hiking, different levels of physical fitness, different levels of physical development, different expectations about being carried, and more.

When planning the hike, try to find a trail with a mid-point payoff – that is something kids will find exciting about half-way through the hike. This will help keep up kids' energy and enthusiasm during the journey.

Generally, kids will prefer a circular route to one that requires hiking back the way you came. The return trip often feels anti-climatic, but you can overcome that by mentioning features you've seen that all of you might want to take a closer look at.

Once you select a trail, map out your route. Using a light colored, transparent highlighter that won't obscure details, trace the trail on your map. This will make navigating the path easier once in the field.

Before leaving on any hike, plan out your trip:

■ Print a road map showing how to reach the parking lot near the trailhead. Outline the route with a transparent yellow highlighter and write out the directions.

■ Print a satellite photo of the parking area and the trailhead. Mark the trailhead on the photo.

■ Print a topo map of the trail. Outline the trail with the yellow highlighter. Note interesting features you want to see along the trail and the destination.

■ If carrying GPS, program this information into your device.

■ Make a timeline for your trip, listing: when you will leave home; when you will arrive at the trailhead; your turn-back time; when you will leave for home in your vehicle; when you will arrive at home.

■ Estimate how much water and food you will need to bring based on the amount of time you plan to spend on the trail and in your vehicle. You'll need at least 2 pints of water per person for every hour on the trail.

■ Fill out two copies of a hiker's safety form. Leave one in your vehicle.

■ Share all of this information with a responsible person remaining in civilization, leaving a hiker's safety form with them. If they do not hear from you within an hour of when you plan to leave the trail in your vehicle, they should contact authorities to report you as possibly lost.

Clothing

Footwear

If a child's feet hurt, the hike is over, so getting the right footwear is worth the time. Making sure the footwear fits before hitting the trail also is well worth it. If you've gone a few weeks without hiking, that's plenty of time for your children to grow, and they may have just outgrown their hiking boots. Check out their footwear a few days before heading out on the hike. If it doesn't fit, replace it.

For flat, smooth, dry trails, sneakers and cross-trainers are just fine, but if you really want to head onto less traveled roads or tackle areas that aren't typically dry, you'll need hiking boots. Once you start doing any rocky or steep trails – and remember that a trail you consider moderately steep needs to be only half that angle for a child to consider it extremely steep – you'll want hiking boots, which offer rugged tread perfect for handling rough trails.

Socks

Socks serve two purposes: to wick sweat away from skin and to provide cushioning. Cotton socks aren't very good for hiking, except in extremely dry environments, because they retain moisture that can result in blisters. Wool socks or liner socks work best.

You'll want to look for three-season socks, also known as trekking socks. While a little thicker than summer socks, their extra cushioning generally prevents blisters. Also, make sure kids don't put on holey socks; that's just inviting blisters.

Layering

On all but the hot, dry days, you and your children should wear multiple layers of clothing that provide various levels of protection against sweat, heat loss, wind and potentially rain. Layering works because the type of clothing you select for each stratum serves a different function, such as wicking moisture or shielding against wind. In addition, trapped air between each layer of clothing is warmed by the child's body heat. Layers also can be added or taken off as needed.

Generally, both you and a child need three layers. Closest to your skin is the wicking layer, which pulls perspiration away from the body and into the next layer, where it evaporates. Exertion from walking means you will sweat and generate heat, even if the weather is cold. The second layer is an insulation layer, which helps keep you warm. The last layer is a water-resistant shell that protects you from rain, wind, snow and sleet.

As the seasons and weather change, so does the type of clothing you select for each layer. The first layer ought to be a loose-fitting T-shirt in summer, but in winter and on other cold days you might opt for a long-sleeved moisture-wicking synthetic material, like polypropylene. During winter, the next layer probably also should cover the neck, which often is exposed to the elements. A turtleneck works fine, but preferably not one made of cotton, as this won't wick moisture from the skin when you sweat. The third layer in winter, depending on the temperature, could be a wool sweater, a half-zippered long sleeved fleece jacket, or a fleece vest.

You might even add a fourth layer of a hooded parka

with pockets, made of material that can block wind and resist water. Gloves or mittens as well as a hat also are necessary on cold days.

Headgear

Half of all body heat is lost through the head, hence the hiker's adage, "If your hands are cold, wear a hat." In cool, wet weather, wearing a hat is at least good for avoiding hypothermia, a potentially deadly condition in which heat loss occurs faster than the body can generate it. Children are more susceptible to hypothermia than adults.

In lower latitudes, higher altitudes, deserts and especially during summer, a hat with a wide brim is useful in keeping the sun out of eyes. It's also nice should rain start to fall.

For young children, get a hat with a chin strap. They like to play with their hats, which will fly off in a wind gust if not "fastened" some way to the child.

Sunglasses

Sunglasses are an absolute must at high altitudes if walking through open areas exposed to the sun, and in winter when children can suffer from snow blindness. Look for 100% UV-protective shades, which provide the best screen.

Equipment

A couple of principles should guide your purchases. First, the longer and more complex the hike, the more equipment you'll need. Secondly, your general goal is to go light. Since you're on a day hike, the amount of gear you'll need is a fraction of what backpackers shown in magazines and catalogues usually carry. Indeed, the inclination of most day hikers is to not carry enough equipment. For the lightness issue, most gear today is made with titanium and siliconized nylon, ensuring it is study and fairly light. While the list of what you need may look long, it won't weigh much.

Baby carriers

If your child is an infant or toddler, you'll have to carry him. Until infants can hold their heads up, which usually doesn't happen until about four to six months of age, a front pack (like a Snugli or Baby Bjorn) is best. It keeps the infant close for warmth and balances out your backpack. At same time, though, you must watch for baby overheating in a front pack, so you'll need to remove the infant from your body at rest stops.

Once children reach about 20 pounds, they typically can hold their heads up and sit on their own. At that point, you'll want a baby carrier (sometimes called a child carrier or baby backpack), which can transfer the infant's weight to your hips when you walk. You'll not only be comfortable, but you're child will love it, too.

Look for a baby carrier that is sturdy yet lightweight. Your child is going to get heavier as time passes, so about the only way you can counteract this is to reduce the weight of the items you use to carry things. The carrier also should have adjustment points, as you don't want your child to outgrow the carrier too soon. A padded waist belt and padded shoulder straps are necessary for your comfort. The carrier should provide some kind of head and neck support if you're hauling an infant. It also should offer back support for children of all ages, and leg holes should be wide enough so there's no chafing. You want to be able to load your infant without help, so it should be stable enough to stand so when you take it off the child can sit in it for a moment while you get turned around. Stay away from baby carriers with only shoulder straps as you need the waist belt to help shift the child's weight to your hips for more comfortable walking.

Fanny packs

Also known as a belt bag, a fanny pack is virtually a must for anyone with a baby carrier as you can't otherwise carry a backpack. If your significant other is with you, he or she can carry the backpack, of course. Still, the fanny pack also is a good alternative to a backpack in hot weather, as it will reduce back sweat.

If you have only one or two kids on a hike, or if they also are old enough to carry daypacks, your fanny pack need not be large. A mid-size pouch can carry at least 200 cubic inches of supplies, which is more than enough to accommodate all the supplies you need. A good fanny pack also has a place to hook canteens to it.

Backpacks

Sometimes called daypacks for day hikes or for kids, backpacks are essential once kids come down from the baby carrier. As the child is older and requires more, you'll need to find a better way to carry all of the essentials you need – snacks, first-aid kit, extra clothing – than a fanny pack.

For day hike purposes with children, you'll want to get yourself an internal frame, in which the frame giving the backpack its shape is inside the pack's fabric so it's not exposed to nature. Such frames usually are lightweight and comfortable. External frames have the frame outside the pack, so they are exposed to the elements. They are excellent for long hikes into the backcountry when you must carry heavy loads.

It's a good idea to get kids carrying a small daypack with a couple of light items in it by the time they're in elementary school. If you don't get them to realize they have a responsibility to carry their own stuff, they'll balk at doing so later.

As kids get older, and especially after they've been hiking for a couple of years, they'll soon want a "real" backpack. Unfortunately, most backpacks for kids are overbuilt and too heavy. Even light ones that safely can hold up to 50 pounds are inane for most children.

When buying a daypack for your child, look for sternum straps, which help keep the strap on the shoulders. This is vital for prepubescent children as they do not have the broad shoulders that come with adolescence, meaning packs likely will slip off and onto their arms, making them uncomfortable and difficult to carry. Don't buy a backpack that a child will "grow into." Backpacks that don't fit well simply will lead to sore shoulder and back muscles and could result in poor posture.

Also, consider purchasing a daypack with a hydration system for kids. This will help ensure they drink a lot of water. More on this later when we get to the water section.

Before hitting the trail, always check your children's backpacks to make sure that they have not overloaded them. Kids think they need more than they really do. They also tend to overestimate their own ability to carry stuff. Sibling rivalries often lead to children to packing more than they should in their rucksacks, too. Don't let them overpack "to teach them a lesson," though, as it can damage bones and turn the hike into a bad experience.

A good rule of thumb is no more than 25 percent capacity. Most upper elementary school kids can carry only about 10 pounds for any short distance. Subtract the weight of the backpack, and that means only 4-5 pounds in the backpack. Overweight children will need to carry a little less than this or they'll quickly be out of breath.

Canteens

Canteens or plastic bottles filled with water are vital for any hike, no matter how short the trail. You'll need to have enough of them to carry about 2 pints of water per person for every hour of hiking. If going into arid regions, you'll probably need more.

Trekking poles

Also known as walking sticks, hiking sticks or walking poles, trekking poles are necessary for maintaining stability on uneven or wet surfaces and to help reduce fatigue. The latter makes them useful on even surfaces. By transferring weight to the arms, a trekking pole can reduce stress on knees and lower back, allowing you to maintain a better posture and to go farther.

As an adult with a baby or toddler on your back, you'll primarily want a trekking pole to help you maintain your balance, even if on a flat surface, and to help absorb some of the impact of your step.

Graphite tips provide the best traction. A basket just above the tip is a good idea so the stick doesn't sink into mud or sand. Angled cork handles are ergonomic and help absorb sweat from your hands so they don't blister. A strap on the handle to wrap around your hand is useful so the stick doesn't slip out. Telescopic poles are a good idea as you can adjust them as needed based on the terrain you're hiking and to accommodate kids' height as they grow.

The pole also needs to be sturdy enough to handle rugged terrain, as you don't want a pole that bends when you press it to the ground. Spring-loaded shock absorbers help when heading down a steep incline but aren't necessary. Indeed, for a short walk across flat terrain, the right length stick is about all you need.

Carabiners

Carabiners are metal loops, vaguely shaped like a D, with a sprung or screwed gate. You'll find that hooking a couple of them to your backpack or fanny pack useful in many ways. For example, if you need to dig through a fanny pack, you can hook the strap of your trekking pole to it. Your hat, camera straps, first-aid kit and a number of other objects also can connect to them. Hook them to your fanny pack or backpack upon purchasing them, so you don't forget them when packing. Small carabiners with sprung gates are inexpensive, but they do have a limited life of a couple of dozen hikes.

Navigational tools

Paper maps

Paper maps may sound passé in this age of GPS, but you'll find the variety and breadth of view they offer to be useful. During the planning process, a paper map (even if viewing it online), will be far superior to a GPS device. On the hike, you'll also want a backup to GPS. Or like many casual hikers, you may not own GPS at all, which makes paper maps indispensible.

Standard road maps (including printed guides and handmade trail maps) show highways and locations of cities and parks. Maps included in guidebooks, printed guides handed out at parks, and that are hand drawn tend to be designed like road maps and often carry the same positives and negatives.

Topographical maps give contour lines and other important details for crossing a landscape. You'll find them invaluable on a hike into the wilds. The contour lines' shape and their spacing on a topo map show the form and steepness of a hill or mountains, unlike the standard road map and most brochures and handmade trail maps. You'll also know if you're in a woods, which is marked in green, or in a clearing, which is marked in white. If you get lost, figuring out where you are and how to get to where you need to be will be much easier with such information.

Satellite photos offer a view from above that is rendered exactly as it would look from an airplane. Thanks to Google and other online services, you can get fairly detailed pictures of the landscape. Such pictures are an excellent resource when researching a hiking trail. Unfortunately, those pictures don't label what a feature is or what it's called, as would a topo map. Unless there's a stream, determining if a feature is a canyon bottom or a ridgeline also can be difficult. Like topo maps, satellite photos (most of which were taken by old Russian spy satellites), can be out of date a few years. Google satellite photos aren't in real time.

GPS

By using satellites, the global positioning system can find your spot on the Earth to within 10 feet. With a GPS device, you can preprogram the trailhead location and mark key turns and landmarks as well as the hike's end point. This mobile map is a powerful technological tool that almost certainly ensures you won't get lost – so long as you've correctly programmed the information. GPS also can calculate travel time and act as a compass, a barometer and altimeter, making such devices virtually obsolete on a hike.

In remote areas, however, reception is spotty at best for GPS, rendering your mobile map worthless. A GPS device also runs on batteries, and there's always a chance they will go dead. Or you may drop your device, breaking it in the process. Their screens are small, and sometimes you need a large paper map to get a good sense of the natural landmarks around you.

Compass

Like a paper map, a compass is indispensible even if you use GPS. Should your GPS no longer function, the compass then can be used to tell you which direction you're heading. A protractor compass is best for hiking. Beneath the compass needle is a transparent base with lines to help your orient yourself. The compass often serves as a magnifying glass to help you make out map details. Most protractor compasses also come with a lanyard for easy carrying.

Food and water

Water

As water is the heaviest item you'll probably carry, there is a temptation to not take as much as one should. Don't skimp on the amount of water you bring, though; after all, it's the one thing your body most needs. It's always better to end up having more water than you needed than to return to your vehicle dehydrated.

How much water should you take? Adults need at least a quart for every two hours hiking. Children need to drink about a quart every two hours of walking and more if the weather is hot, dry or cold and if at a high altitude. To keep kids hydrated, have them drink at every rest stop.

Don't presume there will be water on the hiking trail. Most trails outside of urban areas lack such public amenities. In addition, don't drink water from local streams, lakes, rivers or ponds. There's no way to tell if local water is safe or not. As soon as you have drunk half of your water supply, you should turn around for the vehicle.

Milk for infants

If you have an infant or unweaned toddler with you, milk is as necessary as water. Children who only drink breastfed milk but don't have their mother on the hike require that you have breast-pumped milk in an insulated beverage container (such as a Thermos) that can keep it cool to avoid spoiling. Know how much the child drinks and at what frequency so you can bring enough. You'll also need to carry the child's bottle and feeding nipples. Bring enough extra water in your canteen so you can wash out the bottle after each feeding. A handkerchief can be used to dry bottles between feedings.

Don't forget the baby's pacifier. Make sure it has a string and hook on it so it connects to the baby's outfit and isn't lost.

Food

Among the many wonderful things about hiking, at least for the kids, is that snacking between meals isn't frowned upon. Unless going on an all-day hike in which you'll picnic along the way, you want to keep them fed, as hungry children can lead to lethargy and whininess. It'll also keep young kids from snacking on the local flora or dirt. Before hitting the trail, you'll want to repackage as much of the food as possible as products sold at grocery stores tend to come in bulky packages that take up space and add a little weight to your backpack. Place the food in re-sealable plastic bags.

Bring a variety of small snacks for rest stops. You don't want kids filling up on snacks, but you do need them to maintain their energy levels if they're walking or to ensure they don't turn fussy if riding in a baby carrier. Go for complex carbohydrates and proteins for maintaining energy. Good options include dried fruits, jerky, nuts, peanut butter, prepared energy bars, candy bars with a high protein content (nuts, peanut butter), crackers, raisins and trail mix (called "gorp"). A number of trail mix recipes are available online; you and your children may want to try them out at home to see which ones you collectively like most.

Salty treats rehydrate better than sweet treats do. Chocolate and other sweets are fine if they're not all that's exclusively served, but remember they also tend to lead to thirst and to make sticky messes. Whichever snacks you choose, don't experiment with food on the trail. Bring what you know kids will like.

Give the first snack within a half-hour of leaving the trailhead or you risk children becoming tired and whiny from low energy levels. If kids start asking for them every few steps even after having something to eat at the last rest stop, consider timing snacks to reaching a seeable landmark, such as, "We'll get out the trail mix when we reach that bend up ahead."

What not to bring

Avoid soda and other caffeinated beverages, alcohol, and energy pills. The caffeine will dehydrate children as well as you. Alcohol has no place on the trail; you need your full faculties when making decisions and driving home. Energy pills essentially are a stimulant and like alcohol can lead to bad calls. If you're tired, get some sleep and hit the trail another day.

First-aid kit

After water, this is the most essential item you can

carry.

A first-aid kit should include:

■ Adhesive bandages of various types and sizes, especially butterfly bandages (for younger kids, make sure they're colorful kid bandages)

■ Aloe vera

■ Anesthetic (such as Benzocaine)

■ Antacid (tablets)

■ Antibacterial (aka antibiotic) ointment (such as Neosporin or Bacatracin)

■ Anti-diarrheal tablets (for adults only, as giving this to a child is controversial)

■ Anti-itch cream or calamine lotion

■ Antiseptics (such as hydrogen peroxide, iodine or Betadine, Mercuroclear, rubbing alcohol)

■ Baking soda

■ Breakable (or instant) ice packs

■ Cotton swabs

■ Disposable syringe (w/o needle)

■ Epipen (if children or adults have allergies)

■ Fingernail clippers (your multi-purpose tool might have this, and if so you can dispense with it)

■ Gauze bandage

■ Gauze compress pads (2x2 individually wrapped pad)

■ Hand sanitizer (use this in place of soap)

■ Liquid antihistamine (not Benadryl tablets, however, as children should take liquid not pills; be aware that liquid antihistamines may cause drowsiness)

■ Medical tape

■ Moisturizer containing an anti-inflammatory

■ Mole skin

■ Pain reliever (a.k.a. aspirin; for children's pain relief, use liquid acetaminophen such Tylenol or liquid ibuprofen; never give aspirin to a child under 12)

■ Poison ivy cream (for treatment)

■ Poison ivy soap

■ Powdered sports drinks mix or electrolyte additives

■ Sling

■ Snakebite kit

■ Thermometer

■ Tweezers (your multi-purpose tool may have this allowing you to dispense with it)

■ Water purification tablets

If infants are with you, be sure to also carry teething ointment (such as Orajel) and diaper rash treatment.

Many of the items should be taken out of their store packaging to make placement in your fanny pack or backpack easier. In addition, small amounts of some items – such as baking soda and cotton swabs – can be placed inside re-sealable plastic bags, since you won't need the whole amount purchased.

Make sure the first-aid items are in a waterproof container. A re-sealable plastic zipper bag is perfectly fine. If you hike in a humid climate like the Midwest or Southeast, be sure to replace the adhesive bandages every couple of months, as they can deteriorate in the moistness. Also, check your first-aid kit every few trips and after any hike in which you've just used it, so that you can replace used components and to make sure medicines haven't expired.

If you have older elementary-age kids and teenagers who've been trained in first aid, giving them a kit to carry as well as yourself is a good idea. Should they find themselves lost or if you cannot get to them for a few moments, the kids might need to provide very basic first aid to one another.

Family dog

Dogs are part of the family, and kids will want to share the hiking experience with them. In turn, dogs will have a blast on the trail, some larger dogs can be used as Sherpas, and others will defend against threatening animals.

But there is a downside to dogs. Many will chase animals and so run the risk of getting lost or injured. In addition, a doggy bag will have to be carried for dog pooh – yeah, it's natural, but inconsiderate to leave for other hikers to smell and for their kids to step in. In addition, most dogs almost always will lose a battle against a threatening animal, so there's a price to be paid for your safety.

Many places where you'll hike solve the dilemma for you as dogs aren't allowed on the trails. Dogs are verboten on national parks trails but usually permitted on those in national forests. Always check with the park ranger before heading to the trail.

If you can bring a dog, make sure it is well behaved and friendly to others. You don't need your dog biting another hiker while unnecessarily defending its family.

Rules of the Trail

Ah, the woods or wide open desert, peaceful and quiet, not a single soul around for miles. Now you and your children can do whatever you want.

Not so fast.

Act like wild animals on a hike, and you'll destroy the very aspects of the wilds that make them so attractive. Act like wild animals, and you're likely to end up back in civilization, specifically in an emergency room. And there are other people around. Just as you would wish them to treat you courteously, so you and your children should do the same for them.

Let's cover how to act civilized out on the wilds.

Minimize damage to your surroundings

When in the wilds, follow the maxim of "Leave no trace." Obviously, you shouldn't toss litter on the ground, start rockslides, or pollute water supplies. How much is damage and how much is good-natured exploring is a gray area, of course. Most serious backpackers will say you should never pick up objects, break branches, throw rocks, pick flowers, and so on – the idea is not to disturb the environment at all. Good luck getting a four-year-old to think like that. The good news is a four-year-old won't be able to throw around many rocks or break many branches.

Still, children from the beginning should be taught to respect nature and to not destroy their environment. While you might overlook a preschooler hurling rocks into a puddle, they can be taught to sniff rather than pick flowers. As they grow older, you can teach them the value of leaving the rock alone. Regardless of age, don't allow children to write on boulders or carve into trees.

Many hikers split over picking berries. To strictly abide by the "minimize damage" principle, you wouldn't pick any berries at all. Kids, however, are likely to find great pleasure in eating blackberries, currants, and thimbleberries as ambling down the trail. Personally, I don't see any probably enjoying a few berries if the long-term pay-off is a respect and love for nature. To minimize damage, teach them to only pick berries they can reach from the trail so they don't trample plants or deplete food supplies for animals. They also should only pick what they'll eat.

Collecting is another issue. In national and most state and county parks, taking rocks, flower blossoms and even pine cones is illegal. Picking flowers moves many species, especially if they are rare and native, one step closer to extinction. Archeological ruins are extremely fragile, and even touching them can damage a site.

But on many trails, especially gem trails, collecting is part of the adventure. Use common sense – if the point of the trail is to find materials to collect, such as a gem trail, take judiciously, meaning don't overcollect. Otherwise, leave it there.

Sometimes the trail crosses private land. If so, walking around fields, not through them, always is best or you could damage a farmer's crops.

Pack out what you pack in

Set the example as a parent: Don't litter yourself; whenever stopping, pick up whatever you've dropped; and always require kids to pick up after themselves when they litter. In the spirit of "Leave no trace," try to leave the trail cleaner than you found it, so if you come across litter that's safe to pick up, do so and bring it back to a trash bin in civilization. Given this, you may want to bring a plastic bag to carry out garbage.

Picking up litter doesn't just mean gum and candy

wrappers but also some organic materials that take a long time to decompose and aren't likely to be part of the natural environment you're hiking. In particular, these include peanuts shells, orange peelings and eggshells.

Burying litter, by the way, isn't viable. Either animals or erosion soon will dig it up, leaving it scattered around the trail and woods.

Stay on the trail

Hiking off trail means potentially damaging fragile growth. Following this rule not only ensures you minimize damage but is also a matter of safety. Off trail is where kids most likely will encounter dangerous animals and poisonous plants. Not being able to see where they're stepping also increases the likelihood of falling and injuring themselves. Leaving the trail also raises the chances of getting lost.

Staying on the trail further means staying out of caves, mines or abandoned structures you may encounter. They are usually dangerous places and wild animals may be living there.

In addition, never let children take a shortcut on a switchback trail. Besides putting them on steep ground upon which they could slip, their impatient act will cause the switchback to erode.

While we're not doing an adult hike, anymore, we do remain parents, and as such we must remain alert at all times. Hiking can be dangerous, but only when we fail to be safe.

For more about these topics and many others, pick up

the predecessor to this book, "Hikes with Tykes: A Practical Guide to Day Hiking with Kids." Have fun on the trail!

Part I: Preparing for the Hike Games and Activities

Most children will find fun the idea of a hike and explore. Still, kids can be fickle creatures. Their lack of knowledge and experience in the world often makes them cautious about suggested activities. And in today's video game-oriented, 300-cable channel, Internet-connected world, some kids may be reluctant – or even afraid – to get outside.

You want to sway kids to at least entertain the notion that a hike might be fun. If they hit the trail thinking a long stretch of boredom awaits them, they'll make the experience miserable for both themselves and for you.

In this section, we'll explore some easy steps any mom, dad or grandparent can take to get their kids excited about being outside.

Chapter 1: Getting Reluctant Kids Excited about the Hike

The keys to getting children interested in an upcoming hike is to make it sound fun and to diminish children's fear of the unknown. To achieve this, you can use a lot of different approaches, from getting them involved in organizing the expedition to engaging them in enjoyable activities that makes them more familiar with what hiking is all about.

Coloring Pages

Find coloring pages about hiking on the Internet that you can print for free. Coloring pages showing children having fun and some of the scenery on the trial often gets them excited about the adventure ahead. Type "hiking coloring pages" in an images search engine. Materials: Computer with Internet connection, paper, colors. Ages: 3-10.

Dress Up

Four and five year olds love to play dress up. So why not dress up as a "hiker"? Explorer sets are available at a variety of toy stores or online to outfit your child with such items as a fishing vest, canteen, binoculars, compass, and more. You then can role play a hike by going into the backyard – where your child almost certainly will want to use the cool new toys. Materials: Explorer set for children. Ages: 4-5.

Nature Envelopes

Have children cut out pictures of different objects they might see on the hike: trees, flowers, rocks, animals, etc. Tell them that when they go on the hike, all of you will look for the objects in the pictures they've placed in the nature envelopes. During the hike, have children collect the objects (or a piece of the object) they've found that match their pictures (obviously, they can't collect the animals!). Materials: Pictures of hiking trail or surrounding area, scissors, envelopes. Ages: 4-12.

Read Kids Books about Hiking

Get a library book about hiking, showing all of the fun that can be had on such an adventure. If your library uses the Dewey Decimal System (and most do), you can find hiking books aimed at kids in the 796s of the juvenile nonfiction section. If hitting a gem or fossil trail, pick up a book about rockhounding in the 552s. Materials: Library books. Ages: 4-12.

Entice Them with Online Goodies

Several websites provide a variety of activities and even awards for completing them, all perfectly suited for elementary school children. Some are private companies, such as REI, which offers an Adventure Journal. Others are government agencies, like the National Park Service's Junior Ranger and the U.S. Fish and Wildlife Service's Wildlife Watch Explorer programs. Nonprofits such as the

National Wildlife Federation have mobile apps, games and crafts for kids. Materials: Computer with Internet connection. Ages: 4-13

Check Out Pictures
Show them pictures of interesting animals, plants and rock formations they might see on the trail. Photos taken by other hikers of a trail usually can be found online or in guidebooks. Remember, though, that wildflowers are seasonal and most animals prefer not to be seen, so some of the photos you'll find may not represent what you'll actually observe along the trail when hiking it. You want to be careful of setting too high of expectations for the hike, which is why sticking to exotic rock formations and other permanent features usually is your best bet here. Materials: Pictures of hiking trail. Ages: 4 and up.

Invite Your Child's Friend
If your children are older, allowing them to bring a friend is a great way to keep them excited about the trip. With younger children, though, this primarily is your time to bond with one another, though certainly if you can handle two young kids this is a good opportunity for them to learn social skills while discovering what nature has to offer. Materials: Friend. Ages: 4 and up.

Make Your Own Board Game
Why settle for a video game when you and your children can make a board game about hiking? You don't need much, just some clean pieces of paper that can be taped together (though if you have a large piece of construction

paper, that's better), different colored pencils, markers or crayons to draw with, and some tokens and dice (or a spinner) borrowed from a board game you already have. Using the paper, draw two parallel lines that squiggle around the paper. Mark one end "TRAILHEAD" (this is where the players start) and the other end "DESTINATION" (this is the end point). Divide these two squiggly lines into smaller, equal spaced segments (try to make at least 30-50 segments or the game will be too short). This is your hiking path through the woods. Now add obstacles, such as "Log across Path," "Rock Slide" or "Bear Chases You," writing them on various segments. For the obstacles, players must go back three spaces. Next, add "Gorps," such as "Picked up Garbage on Trail" or "Helped Lost Hiker," writing them on other segments. For the "Gorps," players get to go ahead two spaces. You can decorate the various obstacles and gorps with cartoon drawings or pictures cut from magazines. Players advance the number of spaces that appear when they roll the dice and take turns (Of course, you can modify this by adding "Take extra turn" squares or allowing those who roll a six to go again). The first player to reach 'DESTINATION" wins. Materials: Clean pieces of paper that can be taped together, transparent tape, different colored pencils, markers or crayons, tokens, dice (or a spinner). Ages: 4 and up

Make Trail Mix

Nothing wins the hearts and minds of kids as readily as food. Before going on hike, have kids help you make homemade trail mix, also known among backpackers as gorp. Here are several recipes:

Gorp

■ **Ingredients** – 1 cup salted peanuts, 1 cup raisins, 1 cup M&Ms

■ **Preparation** – Mix in a large bowl. Add other ingredients (sunflower seeds, cashews, granola) as you and your children desire. Portion out.

Gorp Balls

■ **Ingredients** – 1/3 cup each raisins, apple chips, dried apricots, dates and coconut, 1/2 cup sesame seeds, 1/3 cup walnuts, 2 cups peanuts, 1 cup chocolate chips, 1/3 cup honey, 1/2 cup peanut butter

■ **Preparation** – In a large bowl, mix all ingredients, except for chocolate chips, honey and peanut butter. In another bowl, melt chocolate chips, honey and peanut butter for a minute in microwave. Mix the two bowls of ingredients. Shape mixture into balls. Refrigerate to harden.

Kiddie Mix

■ **Ingredients** – 4 cups of Chex cereal, 1/2 cup of dried fruit bits (apple chips, banana chips, or dried cranberries), 1/2 cup raisins, 1/2 cup salted peanuts, 1/2 cup M & Ms

■ **Preparation** – Mix in a large bowl or pour into a gallon-size re-sealable zipper bag and shake.

Ants on a Log

Not technically trial mix, but a great hiking snack for cooler days.

■ **Ingredients** – Celery, cream cheese or peanut butter, raisins

■ **Preparation** – Cut celery into pieces. Spread cream cheese or peanut butter on one side. Sprinkle with raisins, which represent ants.

You can experiment with different ingredients, as well, but always try the trail mix before hitting the trail. You don't to be left hungry in the wilds because you've decided the mix doesn't taste good. Ages: 4 and up.

Your New Assistant Planner

To entice kids, let them help plan the hike. They can assist in selecting the destination, trace out the trail on a map, choose which snacks to bring, and more. Materials: Whatever is appropriate to the planning. Ages: 4 and up.

Make Your Own Hiking Gear

Children also can make their own hiking gear. Trekking poles or a utility belt to hold a water bottle and snacks don't have to be purchased but can be constructed using materials you probably have in the yard or garage. Instructions for a number of these crafts can be found online. Here are some easy ones you can make, maybe even tonight:

Trekking pole

■ **Materials** – Stick, knife for carving wood, sandpaper, wood finish

■ **Instructions** – (1) Walk with your children into your yard (if you have a lot of trees) or to a nearby woods. Each child than can pick a stick that their hand can fit nicely around and that comes up to their hips. (2) At home, carve off bark and sand it. (3) Stain it with a brown or reddish-brown finish. They now have a hiking stick. Most children can't wait to use it.

Water bottle holder
- **Materials** – Duct tape, scissors, water bottle
- **Instructions** – (1) Stretch out a foot-long strip of duct tape, sticky side up. (2) About halfway down this strip, place a second strip sticky side down. (3) Turn over the strips then halfway down the second strip stick a third piece. (4) Repeat steps 1-3 until you have a sheet about three quarters the height of the item to be carried. (5) Fold up the bottom tape's edge and trim the two side edges so they're even. (6) Along the exposed top piece of tape, cut inch-wide tabs in the shape of an H. (7) Wrap the sheet around your child's water bottle with the tabs at the bottom, sticky sides out. (8) Trim the sheet then tape it in place to form a loose pocket around the bottle. (9) To create a bottom for the pocket, fold over the tabs, sticking each one to the next, then cover the tabs with more duct tape.

Binoculars
- **Materials** – Toilet paper tube (two), single-hole punch, markers, wool string
- **Instructions** – (1) Color the two paper tubes. (2) Glue tubes together to create binoculars. (3) Punch a hole in the side of each tube; these two holes will become the back side of the binoculars. (4) Tie one end of the string to one hole and the other end of the string to the other hole; the string acts as a lanyard.

Backpack

■ **Materials** – Duct tape (40-yard roll), scissors, ruler or tape measure

■ **Instructions** – (1) Begin by determining how wide you want the backpack to be; it should be as wide as the child's back. Now cut a strip of duct tape that is about 3 inches longer than this width and set it sticky side up on a clean, flat surface. (2) Cut another strip that is the same size. Sticky side down, lay about half of it over the strip you've previously cut. Now fold over the first strip so that it makes a clean edge. (3) Flip this new piece over and add more strips in exactly the same way until you've created a sheet that is about three inches longer than twice the backpack's height will be. The backpack's height will equal the length from your child's shoulder blades to the top of the small of the back. Make sure the edges are smooth. (4) You should reinforce this sheet with another layer of duct tape by placing perpendicular strips over it. You've just made the backpack's body. (5) Side panels come next. You'll need two. They should be as tall as the backpack will be high and as wide as the backpack's final depth. (6) Fold the first duct tape sheet – the one that is the backpack's body – so that a section in the middle forms the backpack's bottom panel. The other two sections will be the backpack's front and back panels. (7) Tape the side panels to the front, back and bottom sections. Reinforce these seams with additional duct tape. (8) Using the tape measure or a piece of fabric, estimate how long the strap should be so it fits comfortably on the child. Cut a piece of duct tape that it is this length plus the backpack's height. Place another piece of duct tape over it so that the sticky sides are against one another. Make a second strap in the same way. (9) Between the backpack's bottom and back-side and near the side panels and about four to five inches apart, cut two slits as wide as each strap you just made. Thread the straps through these slits. Pull one side of the strap through the backpack's inside and then tape the strap's ends together so that you have a closed loop. Repeat on the other backpack's other side. Then tape the straps inside the backpack to the back panel so that they remain sturdy and strong. (10) You'll next make the flap by creating another sheet, the exact same way as you made the backpack's body. This sheet's length should equal the backpack's height, and the width should be the same as the back panel's width. (11) Tape the flap to the back panel, leaving edges on the front and two panels loose. You can get more elaborate by adding hooks and fasteners so that the flap closes more securely. (12) Tape up any holes and place duct tape over any rough edges.

Utility belt pockets

■ **Materials** – Craft knife, duct tape, scissors

■ **Instructions** – (1) Follow steps 1-4 for the water bottle holder. (5) Fold over the top and bottom sticky edges of this duct tape sheet then wrap it around the item to be carried. (6) If necessary, trim the sheet then tape it in place to form a loose pocket. (7) Close the pocket's bottom with another piece of duct tape and trim the edges. (8) Slip a piece of scrap cardboard into each pocket as a temporary backing (for a stiffer backing, thin scrap wood also can be used). (9) Near the top of the pocket, with a craft knife cut two vertical slits about 1-1/2 inches apart and slightly longer than your child's belt is wide (if a child is making the pocket, a parent should do this step). (10) Slide the pockets onto your child's belt.

Younger children will need help with making their own hiking gear. Ages: 5-12

Play Video Games

What? Yes, there are video games about hiking, usually involving overcoming obstacles you might encounter outdoors or mazes through the wilds. While not as good as the real thing, video games can generate interest in hitting the trail. Kids may even try to re-enact the video games once outside. The White Mountain National Forest and New Hampshire Fish & Game Department offer a couple of online video games about hiking at http://hikesafe.com/index.php?page=games. Materials: Computer with Internet connection; paper; pencil. Ages: 5-16.

Watch Videos

Beat your kids' television addiction by using it as a tool against them: Watch videos, if available, of the area you plan to hike. Usually videos of national and state parks can be checked out from public libraries. The narration can be a bit dry, but sometimes the videotaped scenery is so spectacular that kids want to go there and see it for themselves. Materials: Programs about area where you'll hike. Ages: 5 and up.

Word Finds

For older elementary school kids, word finds (also known

as word searches or word puzzles) featuring hiking and nature terms are available online for free. These are great activities to keep kids busy while you go through the less interesting aspects of planning your hike and can spur discussion as they ask you what a word they've never heard before means. Type "hiking word searches" in a search engine for downloads. Materials: Computer with Internet connection; paper; pencil. Ages: 9-14 and up.

Watch Your Mouth

Don't call it a "hike." Some kids think a "hike" means a death march through boring countryside. Instead, you are going on an "adventure," an "expedition" or a "trek" – or say "we're going to see a waterfall at the end of a trail." For really hard to crack nuts say, "We're walking to a pool where we'll swim." Now from the child's point of view you're not hiking but swimming. Finally, express your own wonderment and enthusiasm about nature. For younger children, it soon will be infectious. Materials: None. Ages: All.

Chapter 2: Driving to the Hike

Once you've got your children excited about the hike, you next have to get them to the trailhead, probably in a motor vehicle. Sometimes those drives to a national forest, nature preserve or state park can be long. You can keep kids' spirits up by playing games on the drive there. Here are a few that always work.

Silly Sounds

Make up sounds to represent certain objects you're likely to see on the drive. For example, when you see a house go "ding dong" for the doorbell, whenever you see a car go "vroom!", or whenever you see a bird go "tweet tweet." Whenever passing these objects, whoever sees them makes the silly sound. Soon your car will be full of silly sounds and laughter. There's no object to the game other than to have fun, but it's a great way to develop pre-schoolers' observation and memory skills. Materials: None. Ages: 3-6.

I Spy "Beep!"

This is a variation of the classic car trip "I Spy" game. Looking out the window, one person in the vehicle selects an object that is commonly repeated – a green sign if on the freeway, a light post, a blue car – and says "Beep!" whenever the vehicle passes it. All others in the vehicle, going round robin, take turns calling out what they think the person is saying "Beep!" for. The person who guesses correctly gets to select an object and call "Beep!" Children as young as 4 can play this game, but you'll need to select a very obvious object. Materials: None. Ages: 4 and up.

Secret Writing

If you have two or more children in a car, have one close his eyes while the other traces a letter in the palm of the first child's hand. The first child then guesses what letter was drawn. For older children, have them trace the first letter of a town or natural landmark (such as a mountain range or a river) that is on the journey, and for a bonus point, the guessing child can name the place. Have tweens trace out each letter of a word. Materials: None. Ages: 6 and up.

Your New Chief Navigator

Have kids learn how to read maps by navigating for you. They can provide instructions about when and which way to turn, for example, by reading a road map, atlas or a printout you make from an online map service. Older elementary school children can answer more complex questions, such as "How many miles are we from (our destination)?" or "What is the name of that mountain range?" Familiarize yourself with the map beforehand, though, so that you know when you're getting bad directions! Materials: Maps. Ages: 8 and up.

Quick Draw Words

This essentially is a word association game. Going round

robin, have one player say a word, such as "tree." The next player then must say the first thing that comes to mind when thinking of trees, such as "leaves." Then the next player says the first thing that comes to mind when thinking of "leaves," such as "fall." The fun of the game is the challenge of quickly saying a word and seeing how silly the associations eventually get. Make the game more about the hike by starting out with a word for something you might see on the trail. Materials: None. Ages: 8 and up.

My Aunt Alice

This classic car game begins with one player completing the sentence "I went on a trip with my Aunt Alice and took _____" with a word that starts with the letter A; for example, the player might say "I went on a trip with my Aunt Alice and took an armadillo." The next player repeats the sentence but has to add a word that starts with the letter B, as in "I went on a trip with my Aunt Alice and took an armadillo and a bat." Then the third player continues by repeating the sentence and adding a word that starts with C, as in "I went on a trip with my Aunt Alice and took an armadillo, a bat and a crystal." All of the players continue, going round robin, until one player no longer can remember any one of the previously said words. Materials: None. Ages: 8-13

License Plate Game

Several variations exist of this classic car game. For young children, keep it simple (and somewhat noncompetitive with no score) by having them identify each letter of the alphabet on a license plate (or even on billboards or road signs), starting with A and heading through Z. For elementary school children, bring along pens and printouts of maps showing the states. As children spot license plates from different states, they color in or check off those states on their map. Of course, this version of the game presumes you'll be traveling someplace (such as a national park) where you can potentially see plates from a lot of different states. Finally, teenagers might play an advanced form in which they make up sayings for the letters on a license plate. For example, "MSH" on a plate might become "Mountains Soar High" or "Mom Says Hush." Relate the game to the hike by requiring that the sayings have something to do with nature or where you're heading. Materials: None. Ages: 8 and up.

Who am I?

This is a great game when you have multiple teenagers in a car. One person thinks of a famous person (such as Peyton Manning) then tells the group, "My first name starts with P." Everyone else now thinks of a famous person whose first names also start with P, such as Pat Ament, Peter Graves, and Patricia Nixon. One of them then asks the person who thought of Peyton Manning a question that is a clue about their own person; for example, the player who thought of Pat Ament would say, "Are you a famous rock climber?" If the player who thought of Peyton Manning can say, "No, I'm not Pat Ament," he has successfully defended his person's identity, and the next player (such as the one who picked Peter Graves) goes next, repeating the process. The player who named Pat

Ament is then out. However, if the player who picked Peyton Manning can't defend himself, the next player can continue asking him a question, in the same vein that the Pat Ament player did. The winner is the player whose famous person has not been identified. Materials: None. Ages: 12 and up.

Part II: During the Hike Games and Activities

Generally, exploring and discovery is enough for kids, but sometimes even they can grow bored with that and become restless. Remember that children naturally have shorter attention spans than adults.

Fortunately, there are lots of tried and true activities you can do on the trail that'll keep kids from getting bored. Most don't require any materials, either. All you're doing is giving them attention. They'll walk forever with you if you give them attention.

Don't bring toys and games from home on the trail, however. You want to keep your load light, and the more that your children bring the greater the chance that objects will get lost, forcing you to spend time looking for them rather than hiking. In any case, the point of the hike is in part to get back to nature. If your children want to play with their toys and games, they didn't need to leave the house to do that.

While your hiking games with kids don't have to be about nature, the trail is the perfect opportunity to teach children about the environment and to develop a respect for it. The trail also is a great chance to develop children's skills, from counting and learning colors to becoming more observant and growing their creativity.

This section of the book divides during the hike games and activities into nature-related and non-nature related games. The games and activities are further organized in each category by age appropriateness. Ages given for appropriateness are general. Your child may very well be advanced enough to do the activity at a younger age.

Chapter 3: Nature-Oriented

If hiking, why not play games and engage in activities that develop the child's understanding and love of the environment? The outdoors is a classroom unto itself with the trail your journey through it.

Rainbows
Using the colors of the rainbow, have children identify something they see along the trail that is a specific color; works best for young elementary-age kids. Materials: None. Ages: 3-9.

Tiny Plant
Have kids get on the hands and knees and try to find the smallest plant they can find. A magnifying glass helps them see the plant up close. Materials: Magnifying glass (maybe). Ages: 3-13

I Spy
Name things you see on the trail and have kids point them out to you. List objects that aren't obvious, such as spider webs, dew drops, a crawling bug, or tossing pebbles. Materials: None. Ages: 3 and up.

Magnifying Glass
Pull out a lightweight magnifying glass and look up close

at various objects seen, such as flower blossoms, tree bark, pine cones and of course, bugs. Ant hills are great, and if your child isn't squeamish, turn over a fallen log for a plethora of cool bugs. Remember to gently replace the log as it is a habitat for the insects. Materials: Magnifying glass; if you have multiple children on the hike, buy one for each child or pair of kids. Ages: 3 and up.

Nature Bracelets

Wrap a piece of duct tape, with the sticky side exposed to the elements, around each child's wrist. They then decorate the duct tape as a bracelet, using items found in nature: small pine cones, grass blades, flower blossoms, and so on. Beware that one of the rules of the trail is to leave things as they are. Still, I can't see any harm in pulling up a single blade of grass or picking an acorn off the trail if the end result is a child growing up to love and respect nature. The key is to not start uprooting whole plants or torturing small animals by sticking them to the tape. Also see Tape Collection. Materials: Duct tape. Ages: 3 and up.

Scavenger Hunt

Look for items either using adjectives (find something circular, fuzzy, rough, black, etc.) or make cards in advance. Take make scavenger hunt cards, you'll need cardboard (such as old cereal boxes), crayons (colored pencils or markers also will do), glue, paper, and scissors. Begin by drawing lines on a piece of 8x11-1/2 paper so that you have four boxes going across and five boxes going down the page. In each box, draw a different item you might find on your hike: a rock, a squirrel, a tree, a pine cone, a flower, etc. (or paste pictures of the objects). While researching the trail online, perhaps you can show pictures of the path or area to your children to give them ideas of what they might find. Trace the edges of the paper on a piece of cardboard. Cut out the cardboard backing. Finally, glue the paper to the cardboard. Don't forget pens, pencils or crayons to mark up the card when going on the hike. Materials: None, but if you make cards bring pens, pencils or crayons to mark them. Ages: 3 and up.

Connection Hunt

This game is similar to a scavenger hunt, except kids need to collect items that are interrelated – for example, an oak leaf, an acorn, and a piece of bark from an oak tree all are related. This is a great way to teach kids about cycles and relationships in nature (such as the water and carbon cycles); the older and more cognitively mature the child, the more complex of a cycle that can be explained. Materials: None. Ages: 3 and up

Tape Collection

Give each kid a piece of duct tape tacked to a piece of cardboard with the sticky side exposed to the elements. When the kids see something interesting, let them stick it to the duct tape. It keeps kids looking for stuff to put on the tape and makes for a good conversation starter later. Materials: Duct tape. Ages: 3 and up.

Collecting Craft Materials

Children love to pick up and examine pine cones, twigs, leaves, pebbles and other small items found in the wilds.

Go online or visit your local library to find children's crafts that you might do at home and that would require such materials collected on a hike. Warning: Many parks and national forests prohibit the collection of such items from public lands. Materials: Bag to carry collected stuff, Internet connection. Ages: 3 and up.

Hungry, Hungry Ants

Once you spot an ant hill, see if its inhabitants have a trail of workers leading away from their home. If they do, follow the ants and discover what they're eating. A magnifying glass helps but isn't necessary. Also, don't play this game with red ants that bite. Materials: None. Ages: 3 and up.

A Bug's Life

Turn over a decomposing log or dig up some dirt in a wet part of the trail and examine the bugs living there. This is a great opportunity to teach kids about the important role insects play and cycles in nature. Or you might try to figure out what makes an insect an insect – after all, not all bugs are insects! A magnifying glass helps children better see the little critters. Remember to replace the log and dirt when done looking. Also, beware that some children may be a little squeamish with what they see. Materials: Spade, magnifying glass (both optional). Ages: 3 and up.

Butterfly Net

Once you start seeing butterflies in your yard, consider bringing a butterfly net on the trail. Catching the butterflies is a fun challenge for kids, and if you bring a magnifying glass to look at what you've caught, can make for some literally eye-popping discoveries. Materials: Butterfly net, magnifying glass. Ages: 5 and up.

Counting

Working in pairs or as individuals, each team or person counts the number of some object they name in advance – squirrels, dead trees, lizards, oak trees, etc. The object sought should not be extremely common, such as rocks or ants, so that teams have to keep an eye out for them. Whichever team finds the most of their sought object wins. Materials: None. Ages: 5 and up.

Finding Patterns

Nature is full of patterns, from the shape of flower petals to the coloring of butterfly wings. Have your children identify different shapes and designs they notice on the trail. Materials: None. Ages: 5 and up.

Grab Bag

Have kids collect in a paper bag objects they see on the ground along the trail. At a rest stop, have them exchange bags. They can put their hands into the bag but not look. Using their sense of touch, have them identify the object. Be sure to return the objects to the ground when done. Materials: Paper or plastic bags. Ages: 5 and up.

Balancing Act

Find something on the trail that can be placed on a child's head – a leaf, a pine cone flattened on one side – and see how far your child can walk with it atop them. You can turn it into a fun competition by seeing who can cross a finish line without the leaf or pine cone from falling off their head. Materials: Leaf or pine cone flattened on one side. Ages: 5 and up.

Memory

Discretely collect 10 objects found on the ground – a pine cone, small rock, fallen leaf, etc. – and cover them with a bandana or other material. Uncovering the found objects, give the kids 10 seconds to see them. Cover the objects; the kids have a minute to find as many of them as they can. The child with the most matches wins. Materials: Covering, objects along trail. Ages: 5 and up.

Nature Bingo

Before going on the hike, have the kids brainstorm about what they might see on the hike: trees, lizards, dragonflies, puddles, pine cones, etc. Have each one make a bingo card with those objects on them (See "Scavenger Hunt" in this section); you can modify the card to become a bingo rather than scavenger game. You'll need to draw five boxes across rather than four. Mark the very center box as "FREE." When they see each object on the trail, they mark it off on their card. The first one to get a line of words across, down or diagonally, wins. Materials: Bingo cards, pencils (or pen or crayon). Ages: 5 and up.

Sniff It

As with grab bag, have kids collect in a bag objects they see on the ground along the trail. At a rest stop, have them exchange bags. They then close their eyes, pull an object from bag, sniff, and try to identify it. Be sure to return the objects to the ground when done. Materials: Paper or plastic bags. Ages: 5 and up.

Spin and Count

To kill time when at a rest stop, have kids spin around three times and count the number of trees they see as spinning. Materials needed: None. Ages: 5 and up.

When You Hear Train

Have children line up single file, then pick a sound, such as a bird singing or a snapped twig. When the person in the lead hears it, that person goes to the back. The goal is to not be at the front of the line when the group reaches a certain destination. Works best with a group of young elementary school kids. Materials: None. Ages: 5 and up.

Who Lives Here?

When seeing various nests and holes in the ground and trees, try to guess what kind of animal might live there. Hang around long enough, and you may see a lizard, bug or furry critter scamper into or out of it. Don't place hands or sticks into holes, though, to force out the animal. Besides disturbing the animals, this can be very dangerous, leading to bites. Ages: 5 and up.

ABCs

Starting with the letter A, identify something on the trail that begins with that letter then move on to the next one. Works best with older elementary age kids with a broad enough vocabulary. Materials: None. Ages: 8-12.

Senses

Have kids tell what they see, smell, hear and touch. "Taste" usually doesn't count and be careful of kids using "see" exclusively. Encourage their use of the various senses by exposing them to various objects. Crush pine needles in your hand and let them smell it, have them stick their finger into an evergreen's sap, have them hold two very different kinds of but similarly sized rocks and tell you which one is smoother or heavier. Materials: Objects found on the trail. Ages: 8 and up.

Signs of Wildlife

Have children point out tracks, feathers, fur on fence posts, scat, scratches on trees, nests, burrow holes, etc. Older kids can speculate what animal might have left it there and then give reasons why they suspect that creature. Materials: None. Ages: 8 and up.

Bark Rubbings

If walking through a forest, have children keep a record of the different trees encountered with bark rubbings. Place a piece of paper over each tree and rub an unwrapped crayon sideways over it. Later use a tree identification guide to see what kind of tree it is. You'll need to bring paper and crayons. As an alternative, or in addition to bark, they can make rubbings of leaves that have fallen from the tree. Materials: Crayons, paper. Ages: 10 and up.

Be the Animal

This is a great game for when some of the group needs to rest but others still have energy. Have the energetic kids get down on their knees like a low-lying animal would and tell how their perspective of what they can and cannot see changes. Then have them climb atop a boulder, pretend they are a bird, and again tell about their change in perspective. Next have them crouch and tell about that perspective. You may want them to focus on a single, prominent object in the distance. Materials: None. The game can be played by children as young as preschoolers if they simply pretend to be an animal. Ages: 10 and up.

Identify Animals

Bring a kid-friendly field guide and see how many animals you can identify on the trail; most of the animals you see will be birds and insects, though if in the Southwest, lizards also will be in abundance. This also is best for older kids. Materials: Field guide. Ages: 10 and up.

Identify Trees and Other Plants

A field guide can be brought along for older kids. If there is more than one child on the hike, see who can correctly identify the most. Materials: Field guide. Ages: 10 and up.

Rest Stop Referee

Have your child keep track with a watch how long you've walked and call out "Rest Stop" when you reach the 15-minute or 30-minute mark. If heading up a mountain, use an altimeter, requiring a brief rest stop every 100 meters. Materials: Watch or altimeter. Ages: 10 and up.

Whichever Way the Wind Blows

If there is a slight breeze, have your children identify

which way the wind is blowing. Then have them identify ways that they can determine its direction (the way trees, bushes and grass are bending, the way a piece of paper bends when held up in the air, etc.). Materials: None needed. Ages: 10 and up.

Sound Map

During a rest stop, have children close their eyes and listen to sounds. Using whatever symbols they like for each sound heard, they then create a map of where those noises are located. After they open their eyes, have them listen for the sounds again. Is the map more "accurate" with their eyes open or shut? Materials: Paper, pencil. Ages: 10 and up.

Geocaching

The fun of this game is using GPS and orienteering to find a treasure. Enter "geocaching" into a search engine and find out what the pastime is all about and how to get involved locally. For older kids, it's a great way to turn the hike into a hunt. Materials: GPS, printout of search instructions, an item to add to the treasure. Ages: 12 and up.

Identify Tracks

Find a kid-friendly field guide or brochure from a local nature center that shows tracks animals make in the region you're hiking. Best for older kids. Materials: Field guide or brochure. Ages: 12 and up.

Animal Track Casting

Once you find an animal track, make a plaster of Paris cast

of it. Using a strip of poster board, form a circle around the track, paper clipping the two ends together. Add water to the plaster in a bag, mixing and squeezing it until it has the consistency of a thick malt. Pour the plaster over the track, ensuring it covers about half-inch deep the area surrounded by the poster board. Let the plaster harden for about 15 minutes. Pull up (carefully!) the cast, peeling off the poster board strip. Brush off any dirt or grass on the casting. Be forewarned that you'll need to carry a number of materials with you to make the casting, so you might want to do this near the trailhead. Materials: About 2 cups of plaster of Paris carried in a large re-sealable bag, poster board strip (about 2 inches wide and 15-20 inches long), paper clips (two work best), bottle of water. Ages: 12 and up.

Orienteering

Have kids look at a topographical map and identify the real world features: a ridgeline, a draw, a distant mountain peak, a stream. With a compass and map, have them track your course on the trail, telling you when you've reached specific points that you've marked on the map. To help kids understand how many steps they need to take to travel a specific distance, they may want to wear a small pedometer. For older children who know how to read a map and use a compass, set a flag hundred yards off the trail, mark on a map where it is, and have the teens try to find it; be forewarned that this does involve going off the trail, and bushwhacking is not recommended for young children. Materials: Topo map and compass brought as navigational tools; possibly a flag. Ages: 12 and up.

Picture Hunt

If you have older elementary school children and each has a digital camera, play a game in which each must snap pictures of as many plants and animals as possible and then correctly identify them. The game assumes that you as the referee and judge know what the plants and animals are. If the park you visit offers a brochure listing common flora and fauna in the area, that list could serve as a guide – or your children might snap pictures of those listed plants and animals in a sort of scavenger hunt. Materials: Digital cameras, brochure. Ages: 12 and up.

Treehugger

After your children have learned to identify some trees, you can play this game to hone their skills. Call out the name of a tree – maple, birch, pine, oak, etc. – and the first child to point it out wins that round. Whoever nabs the most rounds out of 10 is the overall winner. Materials: None. Ages: 12 and up.

Drawing

If your child likes to draw, take a rest stop and let them sketch what they see. This typically works better with teenagers. Materials: Colored pencils, small sketch pad. Ages: 14 and up.

Journaling

If your child likes to write, the outdoors can be an inspiring place to put pen to paper. They might keep nature journals, writing about what they've observed on the hike. Materials: Ink pen, journal. Ages: 14 and up.

Rock Climbing

Definitely for older kids, and it means you'll need to lug some extra gear for safety purposes, as you don't want to fall in the backcountry and then have to spend several hours in pain as being hauled back to civilization for medical attention. Gear you'll need to bring: roping, webbing, carabiners, harnesses, belay devices, climbing shoes. It's not in the scope of this book to explain rock climbing, but there are plenty of good books out there about how to do it safely. Ages: 14 and up.

Birdwatching

Early morning is the best time to watch birds. You'll want to bring binoculars for each member of the party so there aren't antsy kids while waiting to look. Good times to visit a park or nature preserve is when birds may be flying over and stopping over on their annual migrations. A bird identification guide can help you figure out what you're seeing. Materials: Binoculars, bird identification guide. Ages: 16 and up.

Chapter 4: Kid-Tested

These activities don't have much to do with nature, but they're sure-fire winners to keeping children engaged in the walk.

Red Light, Green Light
Kids have to move and stop as you call the signal light color. This is a great way to keep the group together and to play catch up with kids who run ahead. Materials: None. Ages: 3 and up.

Sing Songs
Think of camping songs, driving songs, or standards that everyone knows or can quickly learn (such as "This Land is Your Land," "Yellow Submarine," or "On Top of Old Smokey"). Besides learning classic songs and music, kids will develop their memory skills as they learn the lyrics to these varied songs. Materials: None. Ages: 3 and up.

Simon Says
Have kids move in different ways as they head down the trail: long steps, half steps, skipping, sideways steps, hopping, baby steps. Materials: None. Ages: 3 and up.

Tall as Me
Have preschoolers find something along the trail that is

the same height as them, then something taller, and finally something shorter. Materials: None. Ages: 3-5

Animal Clues

In this variation of Twenty Questions, have one of the children secretly select an animal (preferably one that might be seen where you're hiking) and give a clue about it. The other members of the party try to guess the animal to win. If after five clues no one can guess the animal, the one giving clues wins. Materials: None. Ages: 4 and up.

Cloud Pictures

During a rest stop, lie down on ground or lean against backpacks/trees. Look up at the sky and try to find shapes they can see in the clouds; make up stories about what these different shapes are doing in the sky. Materials needed: Clouds. Ages: 4 and up.

Pretend Expedition

Boys find this activity particularly fun. Pretend you are on an expedition, the first people to ever exploring the wilderness you're hiking. Or maybe you're looking for clues as to Bigfoot's whereabouts. Or you might be on an alien world. Or perhaps you're time travelers hunting dinosaurs. Materials needed: Imagination. Ages: 4-10

Color Find

Announce a color and have your child try to find five objects of that color on the hike. If you have multiple children on the hike, turn it into a friendly competition; the first child to identify five objects of that color gets to select the next color. Materials: None. Ages: 4 to 12.

Counting Bag
Each child carries a small bag and collects a single object (pebbles, twigs, pine cones). At a rest stop, exchange bags. Without looking, each child sticks a hand into the new bag and tries to count how many objects are in it. Closest one wins. Materials: Small bag. Ages: 4 to 12.

Catch Falling Leaves
This is a great activity during rest stops on autumn hikes. See how many falling leaves can be caught, either with hands or a cap. Materials: None. Ages: 4 and up.

One Hundred Steps
Challenge young elementary school kids (especially those feeling a little down) to see who can take 100 steps first – you or them. Of course, since your steps are longer, if they keep up with you they should win every time. Materials: None. Ages: 5-12.

Chief Photographer
If you have an expensive or disposable camera, children as young as 5 can become the hike's official photographer. Allowing children to officially chronicle the hike encourages them to be more observant of the wilderness around them. Seeing what your child considers important and beautiful also opens doors to better understanding their personality. While you might give tips about how to frame a photo or handle the lighting (like don't shoot into the sun), don't be critical of their choices regarding the subject

of their shoot. Materials: Camera. Ages: 5 and up.

Interval Training

If on a wide, level trail, this is a great way to keep kids moving forward while distracting them with a fun activity. Rather than just walking, have them hop, jump, leap, skip, scuttle, crab crawl or whatever other moves you can think of for x number of steps. This develops their motor, counting and listening skills. Never run on a trail, though. Materials needed: None. Ages: 5 and up.

Paper Games

With a piece of paper and a pen or pencil, you can pass several minutes at a rest stop having good fun with a few rounds of tic-tac-toe or a quick game of Battleship in which you draw grids that look like the actual board with the pegs. Reminder: Don't litter. Be sure to pack out the used paper with you. You'll also want to ensure you have a hard surface to write on (two, in fact, if playing Battleship); usually a first-aid kit box is solid enough (albeit small). Materials: Paper, pens or pencils, hard surface to write on. Ages: 5 and up.

Through the Looking Glass

Sometimes along the trail you'll encounter fallen trees or tumbled boulders that you have to go around. Excite your kids' imaginations by pretending that it really is a portal entering another dimension. Have kids describe how everything is different in your new universe. You can switch back to our dimension – or to a totally new one – when you reach another obstacle. Ages: 5 and up.

Trail Greetings

Like pathfinders of old, leave messages in the sand or mud for hikers yet to come down the trail. Ask young children how they make such messages (A trekking pole or a stick found on the trail probably will work fine.) then decide what message should be left. Don't carve messages into trees or write them on rocks, however. Materials: Stick or trekking pole. Ages: 5 and up.

Rock Hopping

Pretend the ground is lava or a river containing piranhas. To survive, kids have to hop between rocks. This is only advisable for kids of elementary school age. Rocks must be flat, large, and close enough for kids to maintain their balance. Materials: Patch of rocks. Ages: 6-12.

Superhero

Each child gets to pick an identity as a superhero that make up. Now have the children develop a list of their superpowers then describe their archenemies. You even can have imagined adventures. Materials: None. Ages: 6-12.

Game Show

If you have multiple children on a hike, pick a topic all are familiar with and have each one create two or three trivia questions. Each child then asks a question in turn. Any of the other children may answer. Keep track of who answers the most questions correctly to determine the winner. If the children are older, the topic might be about where you're hiking. Materials: None. Ages: 8 and up.

Twenty Questions

Give the traditional car and camping game a nature twist. Have the child selecting the object to be guessed select something that could be seen on the trail. Materials: None. Ages: 8 and up.

On Time

Give each child a set amount of time, such as "2 minutes, 45 seconds." You then head down the trail about 30-50 yards (but not out of sight of the child). Without looking at a watch, the child must walk to you in the amount of time you listed. If there is more than one child, turn it into a friendly competition by giving children different times and seeing which one arrives closest to the time you gave them. Materials: Watch (for adult). Ages: 9 and up.

Chain Story

One kid starts a story, and the others continue it by giving a line or a paragraph. Some possible story openers:
- "There was an old troll who lived in a trash can."
- "The little girl wiped a tear from her cheek."
- "The monster wondered if he'd ever see his home again."
- "One day the teacher told us, 'I must return to my home planet now.'"

Materials: None. Ages: 10 and up.

Classes

Announce the name of a class of objects, such as "presidents," "football players" or "mountains." Kids then try to name as many people or objects as they can in that class.

Materials: None. Ages: 10 and up.

Find Your Way Back
During a rest stop, blindfold the child with a bandana or handkerchief. Using a zigzagging, indirect route, lead the child to a tree. Have the child touch the tree for a minute. Then lead the child away. Take the blindfold off and have the child find the tree to which they were led. Works best with older elementary school children. Materials: Bandana or handkerchief for blindfold. Ages: 10 and up.

The Name Game
No, not that annoying Shirley Ellis song. Say the name of a famous person – a sports figure, rock star, actress, your favorite environmentalist. Another person in the group must then give the name of a famous person whose first name begins with the same letter as your person's last name began. For example, you might say "Peyton Manning." A good response would be "Mitt Romney." Materials: None. Ages: 10 and up.

Spelling Bee
Challenge each other to spell names of objects spotted on the trail. This works best with older elementary school kids. Materials: None. Ages: 10 and up.

No "Yes or No"
Kids have to make up questions to ask one another, but it can't be one that can be answered with a "yes" or "no." Players don't have to answer the questions; the object is to get kids to think about how they'll phrase a question. Mat-

erials: None. Ages: 10 and up.

Pine Cone Hacky-sack

Especially for teens, a rest stop sometimes can be a real bore. While younger kids will appreciate giving their legs a break as well as a snack, and while you may need a few minutes to check your bearings, many teens with their high metabolisms will want to keep moving. They can burn off some that energy with a game of hacky-sack, though there's really no need to bring the flimsy cloth ball with you. Use a small pine cone instead. If younger kids want to play, there won't be an argument over whose turn it is as anyone can pick up a pine cone. Materials: Pine cone from trail. Ages: 12 and up.

Poetry on the Go

With older kids, give the first line of a poem, such as "One day I went on a hike." The next line has to rhyme to with the first, such as "And saw a bear riding a bike." Materials: None. Ages: 12 and up.

Math Quiz

Ask older children to solve "complex" math problems, such as 8-4+6=? Trying to do these in your head when walking can be quite a challenge. Materials: None. Ages: 12 and up.

Let Them Talk ... and Talk and Talk ...

You just listen, acknowledging what they've said and asking conversational questions to prove you're paying attention and to keep them talking. There's no better way to

bond with your children. They'll remember your conver-
sations forever. Materials: Bent ear. All ages.

Part III: After the Hike Games and Activities

Once you've completed your hike, pat yourself on the back. You've done a lot of work and have taken both you and your children into a larger world.

Before getting home, you may want to celebrate. Perhaps boost everyone's energy with a stop at a restaurant or at a playground near the trailhead, especially when it is in a village or park that you've never been to before.

Such activities make a memorable end to a day hike. To keep kid's enthusiasm charged, "review" the hike in kid-friendly ways. While you really can't do this with infants, most toddlers and older kids will enjoy it.

Chapter 5: Creating Memories

Sometimes the best way to start preparing for the next hike is to take a look back at the one you've just been on. By talking with your children about it, you can gain insights into what they enjoyed about it, juicing your own creativity as you ponder where to go next. Here are some great after-hike activities that can help you get thinking about the coming weekend's trail.

Look at Your Photos

Make sure you've taken photos of each kid and of the best sights you saw. For toddlers, looking at the photos may be all that you do. With older kids, you might play "Where were we?" and see if the kids can guess at what point of the trail you were on using a map. The photos can be made into posters for your family or living rooms, or you can make them into cards sent during the winter holidays. Materials: Photographs. Map (optional). Ages: 2 and up.

Paper Doll Friends

For preschoolers, create a hiking family as well as animals seen along the way that they can use to relive their adventures or to make up new ones, getting them excited about the next hike. Paper dolls and cartoon animals easily can be found through a search engine, printed and cut out. Have your kids help select the paper dolls to print. To get the paper dolls to stand, glue or tape them to blocks that your kids easily can hold in their small hands. Materials: Paper, computer and printer, scissors, glue or tape, blocks. Ages: 3-8.

Go Back

Revisit trails your kids really enjoyed, especially if they ask to go back there. The place is special to them and certain to become a fond memory of childhood. For many adults, revisiting a trial may seem dull, especially given that there are tens of thousands of other ones yet to explore, so to break the monotony, visit the trail in a different season. Materials: None. Ages: 3 and up.

High Point, Low Point

Ask your kids what were the highlights and the boring parts or disappointments during the hike. You may be surprised by what they say. It'll also help you make the next hike even better. Materials: None. Ages: 3 and up.

Nature Scrapbook

Remember when your kids made leaf/bark rubbings or collected small objects during their hike? Have them now make a scrapbook of their rubbings or collection. Staple 10 or 12 pieces of 8x10 construction paper together (Binders or string also can be used to hold the paper together). Write "Nature Scrapbook," the trail's name, and the date it was hiked on the cover. Then have your kids glue their rubbings or collected objects (these objects will have to be thin, such as leaves, flower blossoms, or grass blades) on the pages. Materials: Leaf or bark rubbings or collected objects, construction paper, staples or binders or string, glue, markers. Ages: 4-13.

Nature Collage

Rather than make a scrapbook, get a large, poster-sized piece of construction paper and have kids glue cutouts of their leaf/bark rubbings or their collected objects to it. Perhaps make a map of the trail with the objects pasted where they were found. This collage then can be hung up as a poster. Materials: Leaf or bark rubbings or collected objects, large construction paper, glue. Ages: 4-13.

Award Badges

Young children will love receiving a badge or ribbon for their efforts. Award them, though, not for completing the hike but for positive behaviors they displayed on the trail. For example, maybe one child for the first time successfully read the topo map or compass to ensure the expedition didn't get lost. Or maybe one of the children came to the aid of another who was having difficulty during the hike. Award badges can be made out of paper or cardboard; ribbons also can be purchased. Materials: Badges or ribbons. Ages: 4 and up.

Look at the Maps

Review the map, pointing out the trail you took and where various fun things occurred or interesting sights were seen: "Here's where we forded the stream"; "Here's where we saw the eagles"; "Here's where we skimmed rocks into the pond." Retrace the steps taken, starting with the trailhead. Materials: Map. Ages: 4 and up.

Get Involved

If your children really enjoy hiking, they might like to attend local slide shows, lectures or orienteering courses, usually offered by sporting goods outlets, libraries and bookstores. They also might like to meet other kids who also are into it by joining hiking or scouting clubs in your community. Many such clubs organize group hikes. Most also volunteer their time to improving trails in the parks and wilderness areas where they hike or give back in other ways, such as picking up trash along trails, clearing growth from them, or raising money for facilities and amenities like nature centers. Type your community's name and "hiking club" into a search engine to find groups. Materials: Local club. Ages: 8 and up.

Share Your Hike

Have teenagers post pictures on an online photo album or maybe create a blog about your hike. Just as you researched your hike by going online and seeing what others had to say about their adventure, so others also can learn from your treks. Materials: Digital photographs, computer with Internet connection. Ages: 13 and up.

Save the Trail Maps

Write on the map the day you hiked the trail and store them away in a notebook or file folder. Years from now, your kids may wish to make the same hike again … perhaps with their own children. Materials: Maps. Ages: All.

Index

About the Author

Rob Bignell is a long-time journalist, editor and hiker and author of "Hikes with Tykes: A Practical Guide to Day Hiking with Kids." He and his son Kieran have been hiking together for the past four years. Before Kieran, Rob served as an infantryman in the Army National Guard and taught middle school students in New Mexico and Wisconsin. His newspaper work has won several national and state journalism awards, from editorial writing to sports reporting. In 2001, The Prescott Journal, which he served as managing editor of, was named Wisconsin's Weekly Newspaper of the Year. He lives with his son in Wisconsin.

WANT MORE
"HYKES WITH TYKES"?

Follow this book's blog,
where you'll find:

Tips on day hiking with kids

Lists of great trails to hike with children

Parents' questions about
day hiking answered

Product reviews

Games and activities for the trail

News about the book series
and author

Visit online at:
http://hikeswithtykes.blogspot.com

.

Made in the USA
Charleston, SC
24 November 2012